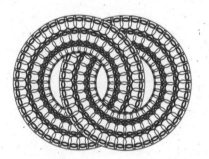

Glitter Road

Glitter Road

January Gill O'Neil

CAVANKERRY

PRESS

CavanKerry Press Ltd.
Fort Lee, New Jersey
www.cavankerrypress.org

Publisher's Cataloging-in-Publication Data
provided by Five Rainbows Cataloging Services
Names: O'Neil, January Gill, 1969- author.
Title: Glitter road / January Gill O'Neil.
Description: Fort Lee, ST : CavanKerry Press, 2024.
Identifiers: ISBN 978-1-960327-01-7 (paperback) | ISBN 978-1-960327-12-3 (audiobook)
Subjects: LCSH: Women authors, Black. | Women, Black—Poetry. | Race—Poetry. | Hope—Poetry. | Life change events—Poetry. | BISAC: POETRY / American / African American & Black. | POETRY / Women Authors. | POETRY / Subjects & Themes / Places.
Classification: LCC PS3615.N435 G55 2024 (print) | LCC PS3615.N435 (ebook) | DDC 811/.6—dc23.

Cover artwork by Harold Fisk, US Army Corp of Engineers, 1944
Magnolia design by Ella O'Neil
Cover and interior text design by Ryan Scheife, Mayfly Design
First Edition 2024, Printed in the United States of America

 Made possible by funds from the
New Jersey State Council on the Arts, a partner
agency of the National Endowment for the Arts.

CavanKerry Press is grateful for the support it receives from
the New Jersey State Council on the Arts.

In addition, CavanKerry Press gratefully acknowledges
generous emergency support received during the COVID-19
pandemic from the following funders:

The Academy of American Poets
Community of Literary Magazines and Presses
National Book Foundation
New Jersey Arts and Culture Recovery Fund
New Jersey Council for the Humanities
New Jersey Economic Development Authority
Northern New Jersey Community Foundation
The Poetry Foundation
US Small Business Administration

Also by January Gill O'Neil

Underlife (2009)
Misery Islands (2014)
Rewilding (2018)

Joy is an act of resistance.

—Toi Derricotte

Contents

I

II

III

IV

V

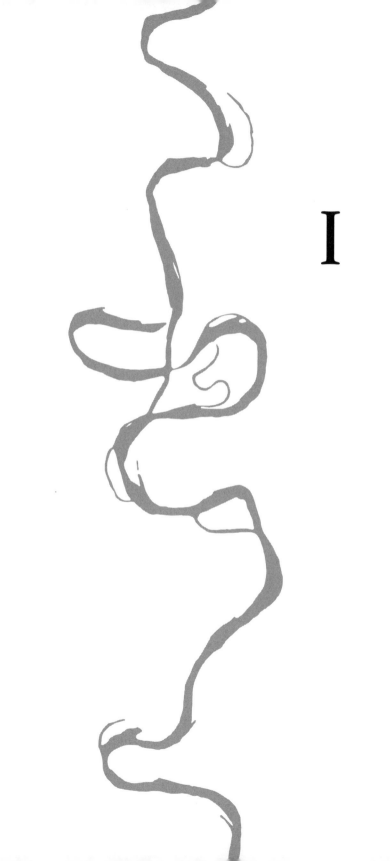

I

Autopsy

—for TPO

I have read the report—inconclusive.
Yet, I know how much your brain weighs,

your liver, your heart. Your ordinary,
damaged heart. I know it by the gram.

I think about the last hands to touch you,
your cool body fully fixed in rigor.

Hospital band around your left wrist,
a tag on your right great toe.

Your eyes were unremarkably blue.
Once, I told you you'd be dead in five years

and I was right. I have forgiven myself
for saying that awful thing people say

when they can't hear their own joy,
when anger becomes connective tissue,

when you looked at me like a stranger,
already estranged from this life to the next.

This is not an elegy or an apology,
the lungs taking in too much water—

this is a memory coming up for air.

What's Left

The scent of green peppers
my fingers keep after chopping, the cool breeze
touching my skin through the open bedroom window,
and the gull flying away in the distance. That flickering
streetlamp across the street. The unpaid bills in the mail bin.
The rain. The leaves in the gutter by the side of the road. Laughter.
A cardboard box filled with old photos, years of Valentine's Day cards
unsent. A single, green bottle cap in the garage. Old fishing lures.
A folded road map you marked with the fastest routes to NYC
wedged in a box with golf tees. And the balls, white, scuffed.
The lobster pot. The wicker picnic basket I could never find.
A broken coffee pot, the last grounds.

Narcissi in January

January in the cold, snowless yard.
January, bottom of the temperature curve.
January, the opposite of July.

A hawk circles the treetops while
a January wind rustles dead leaves
from the great oaks. Noonday sun bright

and diffuse as time. The syntax of strange,
lonely hours. How deep, how often have I
been touched? The knowledge of not enough

crunches like ice in my mouth. January,
from Janus, the Roman god of doorways,
marker of beginnings and endings,

of war and peace. Hard to love.
Two-faced, the coldest month of the year.
January, the first narcissi are breaking

the surface. Green spring stalks bob
their bright white heads, sway in the air—
my name attached to each one.

I Take Off My Black Dress

Lay it on the bed like a corpse,
        unlatch my earrings from their clasps,
            slip on my blue robe.

Hottest goddamn day of the year
        as the AC kicks into overdrive.
            I heat the oven, stuff it

with frozen meatballs.
        Who wants to prepare a meal
            much less eat it?

Outside, the hornets build a nest
        at the corner of the gutter pipe,
            electrons surrounding an atom.

I walk around the kitchen floor
        gritted with sugar. It can wait.
            My son and daughter play house

in the family room.
        We buried their father today.
            From the window I can see the garden

he tilled this past spring. The chipmunks stole
        every last strawberry
            just before they ripened.

Even the dirt sends its regrets.

"What's Love Got to Do with It"

And when Tina sings *I've been taking on*
a new direction directly to camera,
defiant, her lips glazed a tumultuous red,
she takes her hand and adjusts her
honey brown bangs out of her eyes
then continues singing about her own
protection. That MTV moment—Tina
in a denim jacket and leather skirt,
her million-dollar legs in black-seamed hose
wearing fuck-Ike-this-is-my-video heels,
a long way from "Nutbush City Limits"—
indelible on my 15-year-old psyche
when I had no idea what love had to do
with anything—but I understood it was work,
even painful, watching my parents argue
and stay together, years later arguing with my ex
and not staying together. It's only now
into my half-life I can speak of that sweeping
gesture, how the imperfectness of the moment
stayed with me all these years, not as a gaffe
or faux pas for the cutting room floor,
but from a woman in full command of her power,
flaws and all, Tina's hand gliding like the phases
of the moon, that love could be secondhand,
given to pleasure, the rough music
that remains after the light passes through us
because *who needs a heart when a heart*
can be broken.

On What Would Have Been Our 20th Wedding Anniversary

The sump pump breaks, and the ark of my fears
floats to the top of my life. The basement now soggy
with cardboard boxes and busted electronics, headless Legos,
and foam bullets. Indoor puddles rise on the sloped floor.
The green rug that mimicked loam is ruined. For days
the house smelled of failure. We overloved this house,
but didn't understand limits, or high-water tables—
faded salt marks rimming the room's stone walls,
this house with a hole in the floor and a pump-heart
beating the water out. We were swamped, then and now.
I find a dry picture and hold us at Jazz Fest, burnt by the sun.
Soon the day is half gone. When the new machine kicks in,
I listen to its small, reassuring thrum absorbing the silence
of the years, the love I could not save as the muck drains away.

Begin Again

When I welcome you into my house / the carpet vacuumed only seconds before / When I pour you a glass of prosecco / When my son slices mozzarella for his caprese salad from tomatoes we grew / the basil from the garden / When my daughter sautés tomatoes / with pine nuts and mint / Watching her slop red gravy from hot pot to dish is a lesson in grace / in forgiveness / in "that's OK, we'll clean it up later" / When I make a J with my pinky to taste what remains / When you test a bit of crab cake / held together by breadcrumbs and egg / transformed to become otherworldly / uncertainty is the flip side of hope / When I set the roasted green beans in a bone-white bowl / When we take our seats around the crowded table / and face each other / the mismatched plates / the still water / the napkins unfolded / the chatter quiets / When we read Joy Harjo's poem "Perhaps the World Ends Here"/ it is grace / listen / this food is blessed by your presence / When we break bread / together / perhaps the world begins here / begins again / which is no small thing

On the Edge of a Field in Sumner, Mississippi

I pick cotton
with my bare hands
in the town where Emmett Till's
killers were acquitted
in 1955, at the bottomlands
fed by the swollen Tallahatchie.

History of the last empire
explained in its white,
dreamy bolls. Cash crop
so valuable that plantation owners
burned it by the bale
to keep it out of Union hands.

And I can't help but think
about the negro hands,
cracked and worn,
twisting the lock from the burr,
stripping the stalk from top
to bottom, the hard ground broken
against weather and weevils.
Their lives tied to a parcel of land.

Children younger than my own
working from *can-to-can't-see*
under a blistering sun.
Hungry. Half-paid
or nothing. The debts they would
die with. Everything weighed

down to the fiber. Everything
done by hand.

I break off a branch
to feel trauma in my hands—
a reminder that I have risked
so little to be here,
not even the shirt off my back.

Low Delta Country

Driving along Highway 6, I'm not sure where the towns
begin and end. Heavy trees lean ground-close, choked by kudzu.
Roots growing over enslaved land, wild daffodils sprouting across
long demolished plantations and working farms, plots pocked
with mostly unmarked graves. I should have chased that laughter
at the gas station and said hello to whoever stood there
but had nowhere to go but inside. Only-towns, like only children,
carry the loneliness of broken windows in their eyes. They disappear
when the buzzards stop their soar over shorn fields, give up midair,
and drop like a wine bottle. Goldenrod. Deer bones. Billboards
for now-defunct businesses in the town's one strip mall.
Maybe some places should rewild. In the land of John Deere
machines pick clean what the enslaved did by hand.
Irrigation rigs big as pterodactyls sit idle after the harvest.
Tufts of cotton fleck the landscape like cheap insulation.

Rebel Rebel

In the town square where the rebel flag once flew, I buy a faded
green sweatshirt emblazoned with the words *Rebel Rebel.*

My poems brought me to Oxford, Mississippi, a.k.a. the Velvet Ditch:
a place you can fall into, get comfortable among confederate rebels.

A Confederate statue guarded the campus entrance for 114 years. A monument
to grief. To the Lost Cause. Our pain matters less than dead white rebels.

Rebel Rags. Rebel Appliance. Rebel Bookstore. Rebel Wine and Spirits. Rebel
Paintball. Rebel Fever. Rebel Fitness. Rebel Well. Rebel Radio. Rebel Rebel.

Until 2003, Ole Miss's mascot was a plantation owner, Colonel Reb—long
red coat, white goatee, crooked cane. Home games played in the dust of rebels.

Catfish and grits. *Garden & Gun*. Emmett Till's memorial marker
marked with bullet holes again and again and again and again. reb·el:

adjective. 1: opposing or taking arms against a government or ruler;
of or relating to rebels. 2: disobedient, rebellious. Noun: one who rebels.

David Bowie's "Rebel Rebel" is a reverse riff of the Stones' "(I Can't
Get No) Satisfaction." Lightning bolt. Hot tramp. End-of-glam rebel.

Every inch of this place has been touched by trauma. I feel it in the hills.
In the loam. In the wilt of wild daffodils. Who honors the enslaved rebels?

That Confederate statue? Relocated to a Civil War cemetery overlooking Ole Miss's
football field. Athletes demanded a barrier. It looms over practicing young Rebels.

My boyfriend traces his lineage back to slaveholders. His guilt is my kink.
What holds us together is not exactly love. Our bodies rise like rebels.

Magnolia trees splay green and wide in January. So few Black folk downtown,
but the Blues are everywhere. My ancestors walk with me: ghosts and rebels.

Bathtub Graveyard

Past Pirate Adventures Family Fun Center
and the World's Largest Cedar Bucket,
past Dollar General and Cheepo Depot furniture,

past cul-de-sac communities tucked
behind stands of trees, the kudzu kingdoms
and cotton fields along the Purple Heart Highway,

I pull onto the gravel and wander this roadside spectacle:
abandoned troughs in a not-quite junkyard—a limbo,
a bathtub graveyard of cast-iron souls in perfect rows

under the hot rebel sun. Curious creatures
tipped onto their sides, their claw feet
stretched out like dragons.

The porcelain finishes rusted as red clay.
Relics once plumbed-in-place now filled
with stagnant water, ringed with grime lines

of dirt and dead skin cells. Hot and cold faucet handles
stripped or missing, their absence making faces at my face—
tub-spout frowns mimicking the giant O of surprise.

Oprah, who lived two hours from here in Kosciusko,
Mississippi until age 6, has a bathtub carved
in the shape of her body. She says "I spend my time looking

for the best possible bathtub a woman can buy."
How she has learned to cradle her life with care.
I could not have guessed what waited around the curve

of my life: a field of ladyfingers. Giant single slippers.
Cots in a makeshift hospital next to a cemetery with a sign that says,
"Desire is a WAY station between too much and too little."

Today I stop to listen to rusted ghosts—dirt to dirt—
iron hourglasses telling time against a long stretch of road
that will take me east or west, nowhere or home.

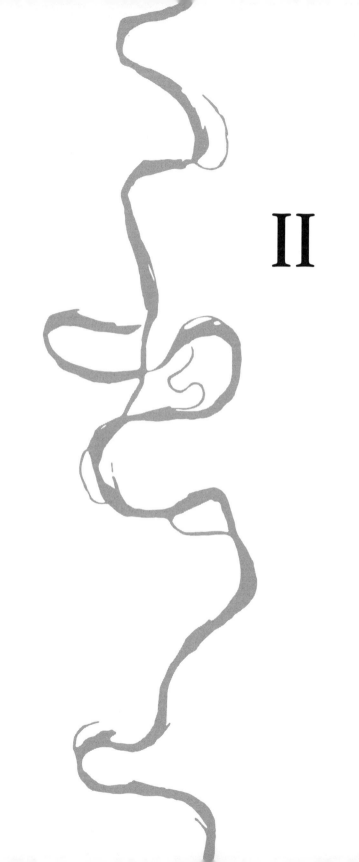

II

Elegy for the End of the World

—After Paul Guest

For the seas, which are rising.
For the coastline: a long necklace
speckled with marinas and marshes,
bays, and inlets. For sea level. Forget
for a moment the distant forecasts,
the inevitability of climate change. This
is for the gulls that wake me at 5 a.m.
with their morning complaint. No restraint
as the darkness ends. Who would miss them?
Who would notice letting go of the world
bird by bird? Show me what I'm going
to lose. For New England, for the frigid
water they say is heating up, but my toes
curled in wet sand don't believe. For the ocean's
ability to clap back. For the answers
staring back at us through sea foam.
For the rocky shores bearded with beach grass.
For the lighthouse at Hospital Point
overlooking Beverly Cove, a mile
from my home, and the bioluminescence
that strands itself on the rocks in late June.
For miracles as neon flecks. For a beauty
beyond beauty, beyond otherworldly,
for the shape of things to come.

Jazzfesting in Place

"If you can't live in New Orleans, let New Orleans
live in you," says the DJ as she ushers in another hour
of a quarantined weekend. First Sunday of Jazz Fest
streamed over the airwaves
                                & just like that
I am back in Crescent City with my girlfriends,
back before the levees broke, back before we knew
who we were supposed to be, dancing in Congo Square
to African drumming, our hearts beating
outside our bodies.
                          Jazz, blues, zydeco, gospel,
brass bands, Cajun. We'd stake out our spot near
the main stage of the muddy fairgrounds
to hear legends: Clarence "Gatemouth" Brown,
Ellis Marsalis, Mavis Staples, The Radiators,
Marcia Ball, Buckwheat Zydeco, Trombone Shorty—
local to the core
                      & when Lenny Kravitz,
in all his funk-filled glory led the crowd in chants
of "Let Love Rule," we became a love army,
our hands up in the air, swaying like
we just don't care
                      while nearby
the big brass of the Second Line marches in:
all suits & horns & feathers & glitter,
a foot-stomping soul parade, the party inside a party,
the best-kept secret, crushed beads abandoned
in the streets.
                      Jazz Fest, where I tasted alligator,

the only place on earth I can find Crawfish Monica.
This giant backyard BBQ where we ate too much,
drank too much, stayed up all night & dragged
boys back to our hotel rooms.

                                    It was one big electric gumbo
in the city where I'd meet the man I'd marry
& dance our first dance on a pool table,
the next day lip-locked in the human crush,
how the rhythm takes over like a sudden downpour.
Aaron Neville sings "A Change Is Gonna Come"
in the Gospel Tent & we are all saved.

Black Women

The news commentator on television says, *Black women*
saved us with their vote. Where would we be without
Black women? He says this emphatically, in high def,
for all the world to hear. Imagine that? To find out
one day we are what's missing, the root in grassroot,
our hearts stuffed like a ballot box as the Suffrage movement
moved on without us. *Ain't I a Woman?* asked Sojourner Truth.
I am sick and tired of being sick and tired, said Fannie Lou Hamer.

My mom would say the times are triflin': Black mothers,
church mothers, night workers, nurses making 62 cents
on the dollar. *In times like this, silence is complicity,*
says Kamala Harris. We carry our communities
on our backs, main streets lined with vacant storefronts,
overpoliced strip malls in stillborn neighborhoods,
gerrymandered and gentrified into spaces so white
they make winter look dark.

America is a miracle, says Yamiche Alcindor.
Being a Black woman in America is a lesson on being.
Caretakers since the diaspora, we show up and show out,
deliver a nation; grieve and reclaim the forgotten names
along the way. We are this country's backbone yet our backs
are breaking. My mom would say the times are triflin'.
What I feel is difficult to name. Rita Dove says,
If you can't be free, be a mystery.

After Daunte Wright's Murder, I Teach a Poetry Class to High Schoolers on Zoom

— for CB

Half the screens—
        half the faces—
are dark.

    //

Another body in the street,
        another death unanswered
by police, some lesser god.

    //

Because I have a job to do,
        I ask students to share their feelings
from writing assignments created days before.

    //

We read Claudia Rankine, Danez Smith.
        Can art effect change when
every bullet blooms the color of elegy?

    //

They write about being invisible,
        about not being seen by the people
who are supposed to see you.

//

A light-skinned girl writes
        she's *the local mixed kid*
who has to prove who she is
        after being told
you're not really Black.

//

(I think about my own biracial teens
        interrogated by this moment.)

//

Another student writes,
        I fear for my dad because he's illegal.
Violence toward AAPI. Black Lives Matter.
        How the small griefs multiply
like loaves in a basket,
        the way resentment compounds itself.

//

Why do the same things keep happening without repercussions—
        protests, arrests, and the same court outcomes?
My students look down as they read.

//

One young man writes
        in that body includes a target.

What is the work of witness

     if Daunte Wright, George Floyd, and Philando Castile

were killed in your neighborhood?

//

(Emmett Till. Emmett Till. Emmett Till.

     His name chimes in my throat like a bell.)

//

My last student writes *our lives matter, too.*

No Joke

Because our candidate—the woman—didn't win.
Because my son is in 7th grade and kids can be cruel.
Because my son is biracial, I did not have the right words
when he came home and told me that some kids said
he would be deported, chanted *Build the Wall*
as he walked down the hall.

They were joking.   They didn't mean it.
My son laughed.   Shrugged it off.

For a moment, I imagined the red lockers
of middle school were listening. Postwar
cement bricks and beige tile bearing witness.

                    My son is not me—
won't carry a grudge,
won't make a fist if not angered. He is learning
how to navigate those halls, to *go high*
        as they say.

But still, I imagine the darker version, the boy
who is not laughing, the deeper physics of molecules
breaking apart, scattering at the cellular level,
whose ears and eyes and hair and skin closed his hand,
felt the vibration of air breaking the light,
who felt broken and broke back.

Proving a Theory

The Pythagorean theorem is one of the few math rules
an adult can remember, my daughter says, quoting her teacher.
I can recite it but choose not to, I tell her, grinning.
Clearly, she is smarter than me—she's one right angle
sizing up the world. She says, *Pythagoras believed that*
every soul is immortal, and, upon death, the soul enters
into a new body—that's why he was a vegan. Duh.
A philosopher with no writings. A stargazer who
connects by relationships, music and numbers
and a harmony of spheres. My baby-girl-turned-
know-it-all. If there is a threshold to understanding,
then maybe she's crossed over. Numbers, irrationals,
the values between values. *Mom, try to keep up,* she says,
rolling her eyes. Too many variables. Too many unknowns.

Cartwheel

And when no one is looking
I will spin my Ferris-wheel-body
into a patch of late autumn leaves,
pretend I am a kaleidoscope
in what I can only describe
as a soul walk,
my neurons navigating
how fast and how hard
I move in space.

I should be dead
or at best badly injured,
fighting gravity in jeans
and an oversized sweatshirt
that flips above my head,
each move betraying me
as the revolution happens.
I have never been a gymnast;
I'm not limber, can't to this day
touch my toes or do the splits.
How have I not broken a bone?
Sooner or later, all our graves
come for us—my legs
cloud-swimming toward
the coming world.

Back straight, tummy tucked,
my stance wide and precise
as I wager a bet on myself.
What I want to say is this:

all this time, I have been able
to balance my little life in my hands.
That I go through the turn
and keep landing on my feet
is a goddamn miracle.

Regret Nothing

If at 4 a.m. you find yourself awake and alone,
curled up in your half-empty bed under a flashlight's

white light reading a poem, little moon
casting its aura across the page, regret nothing:

not the clothes piled in the corner, not the drawers
closed like caskets, the unpacked lunches,

the bedtime story trapped in its book, the child's glove
under the couch missing the body it protects—

all that must be swept, bundled, and carried off
to somewhere else, only to return to the source of your

unmaking. Regret nothing. Even as a glimmer
of yourself catches you in the mirror like a stranger,

walk into the day with your whole heart intact. Walk into
the center of everything. Leave nothing in your wake.

At the Rededication of the Emmett Till Memorial, Glendora, MS

—October 19, 2019

He was 14,
>> same age as my daughter who sits
>>> beside me on the crowded bus.

We travel with police escort
>> like a funeral procession to dedicate
>>> the new marker at Graball Landing.

Along the dirt road,
>> red spider lilies bloom
>>> around the gnarled roots

of aged oaks, life grows on
>> among the silent brown branches.
>>> Delta dust settles to reveal

cotton fields ready for harvest.
>> There have been signs before,
>>> three: stolen, shot-up, tossed in the river—

the last one stood just 35 days
>> riddled with bullets again and again,
>>> refusing us the comfort of leaving

the past in the past.
>> Till's story requires
>>> hardened steel.

This marker weighs 500 pounds. It is black,
　　　　bulletproof, designed to absorb rifle rounds
　　　　　　of white supremacy.

And my heart curves around the side
　　　　of this road, reconciling that old hurt
　　　　　　with an old resolve:

Every time it's taken down,
　　　　it's going back up.
　　　　　　On the Tallahatchie's bank,

we honor; we grieve;
　　　　let our feet sink into the mud
　　　　　　while the brown water rages.

Bryant's Grocery & Meat Market

—Money, MS 2019

You could drive past and miss this place. Ghost-empty,
roofless, its half-walls tentacled by green vines,

foundation fenced in by orange safety netting,
untouched for decades, and I think to myself

this is the place. This is where Emmett Till
whistled at/flirted with/touched a white woman—allegedly.

If these half-walls could talk, what half-truths would they tell?
The family of a juror from Till's murder trial owns this ruin,

unwilling to sell or restore the timeworn remains,
the red letters of a Private Property sign barely visible.

Now weeds grow where the porch used to be.
Shimmer of sunlight turns the window into a mirror.

What's left crumbles under the weight of neglect,
the Delta's way of forgetting its living history.

I stand at a threshold I can never cross.
What's left stays with me, unearthed.

Rowan Oak

The past is never dead. It's not even past.
—William Faulkner, *Requiem for a Nun*

Under beaded lights strung from cedar to cedar,
we dine on low-country oysters: briny and delicate,

salty flesh floating in large shells, shucked and sucked.
Roasted sweet potatoes and spinach salad on the side of this

communal meal celebrating labor: the cooks, the servers, the growers,
the wild harvest, how the fondness of a place triggers nostalgia

and melancholy. On this night, we tread on Southern soil
at Rowan Oak, the grand estate where Faulkner wrote

about postbellum Mississippi. We sit near
his mammy's quarters. Like history, it is in plain view.

Eighty years before Faulkner, the enslaved who lived
and labored here built the university that now owns this space—

a constant reminder that the past is never past.
We drink wine, listen to laughter all night, which sounds

like indifference. The remaining oysters are stirred into a stew,
the kind of dish we made for ourselves, adding what remained

to heavy cream, the grace of salt and pepper. Praise every
complicated bite. Each spoonful becomes a memorial, a reckoning.

I Slept in John Grisham's Bed

—Oxford, MS

A bed on stilts, queen sized, with a well
in the center I'd always roll into. White,
pilled sheets, threadbare and thinning.

I worked hard to earn that bed
and the room surrounding it—meaning,
I must have written words, once,

that meant something. Big wide windows
look onto a cluster of magnolias that never
lose their leaves. No blinds. I like to let the light in.

I imagine John Grisham plotting out a best seller,
yellow legal pad in hand, kids like mine bouncing
on a mattress high enough to touch the ceiling fan.

This bed I have shared with many authors and lovers,
who also wrote words that meant something.
They slept here, loved here, too, on this bed

that scoots away from the wooden headboard
from too much movement. Can't help but laugh
at the bedroom door that does not lock,

sliding a chair in front of it for privacy,
or the attic we were afraid to enter,
the creak of the floorboards above our heads.

And when I'd think my big thoughts about the world—
time travel or black holes or God or death—I'd come
to the bed's blank page against the shimmer of skyglow.

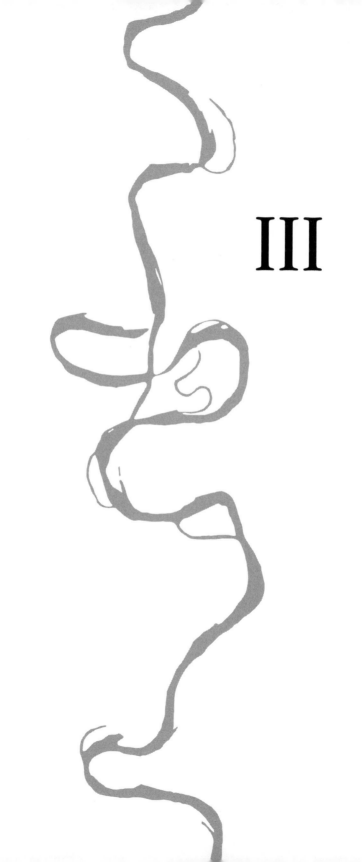

III

In the Blue Hour

I look for the supermoon obscured by clouds,
listen to tree frogs, called peepers in New England,

their rhythmic chirp signaling the start of spring.
Tell me again about the absence of an hour

and I'll tell you what it means to be present.
I tuck a strand of black hair behind one ear,

lean in, listen to another language,
murmur of evening rising.

    //

Evening rises with a murmur.
I lean in, listen to another language,

one strand of black hair tucked behind my ear.
Tell me what it means to be present

and I'll tell you about the absence of an hour.
Rhythmic chirping signals the start of spring.

Peepers from New England? Or are they tree frogs?
The supermoon is obscured by clouds. Look for it.

Elation

In the city's center is an unwalled forest:
a dense plot of cedars so thick their canopy
keeps light from reaching the ground.

We gaze at the stretched-out stalks—
etiolation, you say, pointing skyward,
but all I hear is *elation*.

It's the elongation of stems,
the branches growing up, not out,
their long trunks turned white

from too little light. Tolerant trees.
They claim this space as their own,
making the most of what's given them.

Their back-and-forth sway moves us.
We listen to spindly trees creaking—
rocking chairs on a wooden porch,

the sound of a cello's drawn breath,
the clatter of branches like the chatter
between old, coupled voices

when no one is around.

Woman Swallowed by a Python in Her Cornfield

Inside every woman is a snake. Some think I'm a hoax or an oddity,
rarer than winning Powerball or being struck by lightning. Everything
has a form, even doubt. Think of me as someone you've met in a dream.
Green stalks shade the sun, keep me hidden from the villagers,
the nonbelievers. To find me you must enter me. Oh,
that your body fits into my body makes us unholy. Let me press
my mouth to your scar, run my tongue along your flesh so I can taste
how you wound. The wild boars patrolling the edges won't save you.
Footprints. Flashlight. Machete. Slippers. All that I've left behind.
Inside every snake is a woman. That's the part of me I love the most—
reticulated constrictor, word made flesh, time unfolding, lore or legend,
I am done telling the kinder story. I am a myth of my own making.
Part my snake flesh and you will find me intact, clothed as I was
when I visited the corn. Think of me as the gift you're unsure how to open.

The Beyond Place

Eat for the hunger that comes,
      says our guide, as I try
         my first serviceberry:

purplish globes, sweet
      with an almond finish.
         I am a first-time forager,

marveling this marvel of landscape
      made lush by the rush of the Hoosic's
         underground waters. The name, he tells us,

was translated from Algonquin
      as "the beyond place."
         Generous June. Every tree surrenders

its green flags while
      we crouch ground-low,
         spy the wide splays of leaves,

their dark, papery undersides
      send messages from below:
         this plant is edible; this one will kill you.

I climbed out of one world—
      tongue-first—
         to taste another.

City girl. Chicken of the Woods.
      Yet here the humid wind softens
         the cicadas' strident song

as we root and snip, bend stems
   back to the point of breaking
      to discover wild carrot, or is it hemlock?

Stick with the berries, I tell myself.
   A rough twang, a touch of funk—
      trust the joy I know.

The Morning Before the Rains Came

A coyote runs across the dirt road
and into the woods. Light gray fur,
all haunches and tail. Nuisance.
        I have seen her running once before
like an animal released, breath of
everything filling her lungs.
            Desire or flight?
I could not tell from my car, the windshield
covered in dust and pollen—feeling grizzled myself,
time dilated into clusters and clusters of fallow.
                     Bitch.
My eyes follow her to the curve of road
where the last of summer's sweet persimmons
have fallen, past the abandoned shed where
the native grasses have rewilded
                 and she is gone,

racing against a sky of gathering clouds
toward the sentries of trees standing guard
preventing even the light from entering.

Cheaters

—a duplex, after Jericho Brown

The Stones got it right: it's a drag getting old.
I bought reading glasses to see words clearly.

With my first pair of cheaters, I see things clearly
now that I've reached the half-life of my life.

I've reached my half-life—
should've read the fine print.

Because I didn't read the fine print,
I thought a marriage was forever.

I thought marriage meant forever.
I'm an unmarried woman past her meridian.

I'm an unmarried woman past her meridian
and sometimes I can't help but feel cheated.

I can't help it. I wish he hadn't cheated.
I didn't see the writing on the wall

but the writing's on the wall—
what a drag it is getting old.

Harvest

September, summer's humid sigh.
        I stretch my body out under
                the harvest moon, arms akimbo

as I stand alone in my back yard
        hidden under a canopy of oaks.
                I need a moment without malice,

an hour without doubt or debt
        or death. I need a moment when no one
                wants or needs me, no questions,

no answers, where nothing can eclipse me
        but earth's shadow, silent as an afterlife.
                And I am heavy on the ground surrounded by

brown grass and leaves
        as the first rough acorns of fall
                begin their descent.

The sky is empty of everything
        except the deepest darkness
                and a rising moon. I am thankful

for this minute of pause,
        before gravity pulls me in,
                says, *Begin again.*

Postbellum

I drive down the long drag of highway
past cotton fields heavy with seed,
bolls sagging under the weight of clouds,

where John Deere picks clean
what slaves did by hand—all that's left
after the Great Migration,

where roof-rusted ramshackles
abut abandoned plantations,
and where a tin shack stands, the words "Dirt Cheap"
are spray-painted in large red letters.

In these tumbledown counties
of the small-town South
I never drop my guard,
a lesson learned growing up
in old-South Virginia—
something I knew
before I was born.

At Mississippi's crossroads,
I've come to see what's left,
what's remained unclaimed for decades:
cypress, palmetto, tupelo, river birch.
To love the magnolia and lament the smell.
This place is not finished with me.

Three white Ole Miss students use guns to vandalize a memorial to lynching victim Emmett Till

—USA Today, July 2019

They pose their bodies as if they've just bagged
their first 10-point buck. One holds a shotgun,
another squats below the shot-up sign,

a third stands with an AR-15.
Three faces smiling, hoisting guns
in front of a bullet-ridden marker:

This is the site where Till's body
was removed from the river.
It is hunters' hours.

The sign's jagged holes could slice
a finger. Those students are someone's sons
or brothers, not much older than

the young black boy, his body beaten,
tethered to a 75-pound cotton-gin fan
and thrown into the Tallahatchie.

This is an old story, a Southern Gothic.
To deny this boy's life and then
deny the marker that says he lived

breaks me every time. The camera captures
the night's dark cover, the tall grasses,
the momentary flash

illuminating their shit-eating grins
and the gun barrels' glint—lifetimes
of getting away with it.

Driving Through Mississippi After the Capitol Hill Riot

—January 9, 2021

And when that country dog blocked the car
snarling, put his body in front of the front tire,
it stopped us from passing on an otherwise
quiet afternoon: the winter grass a pale yellow,
new brick houses threading through
a two-lane road on our way someplace else.
That dog—maybe a Feist or Red Heeler—
coat of dark amber, rust dog, all bark all bite, unchained
perhaps for the first time today, would not be moved.

America, haven't we been here before? Standing our ground
in failing light, our breaths held, not knowing what will happen next,
the texture of this moment turning so hard so fast,
that dog flushed with adrenaline and a loud echoing bark,
teeth clenched toward whatever comes down the road.

Robert Johnson's Grave

There are three markers
where his body might be.
I visit the one at Money Road,
down the way from where
the song claims Billy Joe McAllister
jumped off the Tallahatchie Bridge.
Everything here
is ground-soaked in legend.
Delta blues gather
like a rainstorm.

At 27, he played every note
he was ever gonna play,
all those never-played notes
murmur among the whisky bottles
and plastic flowers. I add a penny
to the three on top of his
tombstone.

And I can imagine this kid
at the crossroads:
quicksilver guitar, the drift
of voice over impossible notes,
hands sorting the vernacular
of Blues fret by fret
playing juke joints and street
corners, dying years before
Elvis and Chuck Berry
made rock & roll
king.

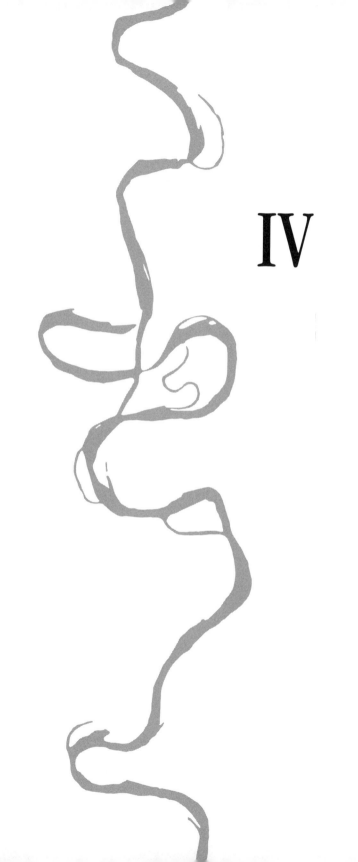

IV

The Great Hello

A big-ass moon rises full and wide
in the western sky. The deep pond

awakens with the tongues of bullfrogs.
I'm barely over the threshold before

our mouths lock and we slither
onto the bed. We watch each other

watching each other with a silent urging,
a kindness for the other in the pursuit of pleasure.

I fling my head back as he grabs my hips,
pulls me close, begin to feel myself levitate,

hovering above the bed as the shadow
of someone I don't recognize but have known

all her life. I am an over-easy egg
trying not to break her yolk,

but I do. The joy of leaving the body,
tender and shimmering. A moment of gratitude

for every daunting thing that brought me to this place
where I am my most fearless, my most true.

I wick the sweat from his head, slide my hand across
his glistening skin before crawling back into myself,

sprawled across the sheets, streaked in moonlight.

Boyfriend Pantoum

Hallmark does not make a card for this
for what we mean to each other,
for what we do when my kids are asleep.
We are not married. Not husband and wife.

What do we mean to each other?
More than lovers, more than friends
but we are not married. Not husband and wife.
One card says, *Know what I love about you?*

Or *To My Partner, To My Friend,*
with the inside left blank.
My boyfriend asks, "what do you
know about me?" as he brings me water at 3 a.m.

With the inside left blank
I write *To the man I spend my nights with,*
who brings me a glass of water at 3 a.m.,
whose body was made to fit inside my body:

There's no one else I'd rather spend my nights with.
Who are we when my kids are asleep?
His beautiful body fits inside of my body.
Hallmark does not make a card for this.

Dark Matter

Tonight I am thankful for whatever cosmic
strings are holding the universe together.

Under a great oak I gaze up at the night sky
to marvel at ghost distortions I cannot see—

ripples in the great fabric of space moving around me
and through me, cocooning the galaxy, keeping us fixed

upon this earth. I breathe in ash or dust
and call it solitude, a practice of self-preservation

now a test of faith that can turn on a dime, a trick
of light, or some ancient blueprint playing itself out.

I need a new theory of gravity that explains
how to claim the world and not fracture it,

an algorithm to decrypt this complicated time
of together alone. Evenings like this bring with it

a kind of quiet that can't be named, my qualms
exhaled out as tiny crystals into the icy air,

swimming in primordial soup, the fine mist of it
an unknowable story, floating toward grace.

Axilla

My wing, my least attractive body part,
the one for which I cringe every time
I lift my arm to shave, or check in the mirror
for lumps. Warm hollow. Ruddy cave wall.
Pulled bark from an aged oak. It carries
the scar from my eighth year when I cut
my underarm on a metal fence playing
hide and seek. The mark that won't fade.

It's your favorite part of my body.
How you'd stretch my arm straight, run your hand
along the side of my chest, soft and unguarded.
You'd tell me how you liked *all of me*: the texture,
the stubble, the sweaty desire, the wild touch.

And for that moment, I believed.

Dragonfly

The dragonflies are totally
fucking, spinning like a Ferris
wheel out-of-control, hovering
as they savor summer's last
gasp. Bluish, electric, their
black lacewings whirl and dip,
skim the pond's surface
but never go under, not yet.
And now it's all I can think about:
the female—a bad Mama Jama—
dictating the dance, seeking
pleasure where she can
with the best flyers. Heat seekers.
Sometimes she lays eggs,
sometimes they mate until
they die. But it's not love.
No time for loneliness or regret.
Such a singular way of being
in the world. I watch the lilt
of their bodies as they loop
in dappled light with a hunger
that says *do it. Get some.*
Wings pushed downward,
backwards, feathering up then forward—
keep her from drowning.

Clit Ode

Peach pit sucked clean.
Cosmic marble. An orchid

in a perpetual garden, or sea glass
brushed smooth by the surf's rough tongue.

Afternoons we wasted as the sun dipped
below the horizon, stretched out on my bed,

my back arched, your mouth made to amaze
as I climb a trellis into the wild familiar.

My mind hovers over the magnolia trees,
the windows, the deep pond, the open field

where I stood sometimes under the stars
listening to a coyote's howl, an aching

in the low light of winter.

From Memory

I miss the way you'd text me at 4 a.m., "You up?" and read me a poem. Usually a Jack Gilbert but sometimes one of mine, as if you were holding a mirror up to my life with the best lighting. *I know a woman who makes heaven out of her body,* and I'd almost believe those words were yours. And sometimes I would wake to the sensation of your chest pressing into my back, how your hand journeyed from belly to breast in one graceful glide. Our luminous, complicated joy, the way it traveled and faded. Sometimes *there is only dark and the familiar place of my body.* There were nights so simple it was as if the stars came down to sit with us, not saying a word. Whatever is sealed between us, memory holds it in place. When I can't sleep, I exhaust myself by looking into the blue night. That star I'm seeing is the light that left a long time ago.

Bloom

An orchid grows inside of me,
blooms from a tight bud
in my chest; its milk-white petals
lean against the wall of my ribs.
Lost breaths, red heart bulging,
steady pulse of my soul shifting
in this incomplete landscape
of light. Loneliness takes root
with a beauty that surprises me,
suggests a kind of comfort,
feeds on everything I am.

     //

It feeds on everything I am,
suggests a kind of comfort,
with a beauty that surprises me.
Loneliness takes root and light
in this incomplete landscape.
My soul shifts, steady pulse,
red heart bulging, lost breaths
lean against the wall of my ribs.
In my chest, milk-white petals
bloom from a tight bud,
an orchid grows inside of me.

On Hearing Mississippi's Governor Declare April "Confederate Heritage Month"

If you say, "this, too, shall pass," then you don't understand trauma, how it seeps into a landscape, where every inch of land has been touched by enslaved hands. I think of a war that's far from civil in a state overcrowded with Old South statues. Emmett Till. Medgar Evers. Freedom Riders. When Nina Simone belts out "Mississippi Goddam" at her piano, she means *here*, a place where the governor celebrates April as "the month when, in 1861, the American Civil War began." This is how trauma flairs in the body—*when white folks catch a cold, black folks catch pneumonia*—a phrase taken as gospel while the governor wants us to "pray it away," while a virus burns like brush through the American South. If you say, "this, too, shall pass," then you forget its music, the Blues, rooted in a struggle as long and flat as time. But sure, let's dress up and reenact the past. The Southern Strategy at work. It's in the blood. It's in the soil.

The River Remembers

Here the water is silt brown,
        stretches mile-wide,
                flat as a washed-out conveyor belt,
        an unhemmed rumble strip.
I can't read the River, can't see my hand
when it plunges elbow-deep
        to feel the cool against
                the Mississippi heat—
        hot as a dog's mouth.
Here we canoe for hours
through swirling eddies,
        watch the trash barges
                and towboats travel downstream.
        The River glistens hard as broken glass.
Here, everything is fluid.
In lower Mississippi, the South's south,
        where the two-lane blacktop cuts through
                an infinity of flat: cotton, soybean, corn.
        Farm, farm, tumbledown shack.
Creeks and rivers bifurcate the land like blood veins.
Here, the GPS gives up.
        New islands form at the current's whim
                and what is untouched grows lush and verdant.
        Willow and privet border the collapsing coastline.
A carp leaps into the boat when it hears us coming.
We stop here in an oxbow, gumbo mud sticks to our feet.
        River rock. Plastic. Fossils. Gar.
                Raccoon and coyote leave tracks in rust-colored sand.
        The slaves—sold down the river—hid here,

waited for their chance to escape up north,
hid in caves, fled to the Twin Cities and Canada,
       their fate at the mercy of the river's next rise.
        Here's the nadir of our suffering,
     which started in one place to end in another.
Here's where flow and marvel and history converge.
This harmjoy. This beautiful sadness.

Mississippi Season

He says I hold my mind well,
likes that I put my kids first
and have never tried drugs.
The lilt in his southern drawl
intoxicates me. He likes
not being able to have all of me,
makes him want me more.
Broken finds broken, I say,
so when he kisses my neck
along my clavicle down
to my breast, I break
all over again
after a drought
of no kissing, no touch.
How not being chosen
can dim any light.
For years I told myself
a story I could live with,
thought of myself
a kind of carnival fish
in a plastic bag
floating in my own still water,
waiting to be loved.
Dumb luck that someone
flips a red ring on the mouth
of a glass jar and just like that,
I am kissing again,
kissing a man so luminous—
so beautifully flawed—

I can barely look at him.
And my mind, done
with all its stories,
turns to the carnal
as I rim the hinge
of his lips with my tongue
and dive into
this quenching.

The Map

—Mississippi River Meander Belt #7,
Mississippi River Commission, 1944

Blues, greens, oranges, and reds shade
the paths across a vintage map of The Mississippi,
a birthday gift. Backswamps and braided streams
loop the river channels thousands of years old,
a cacophony of overlapping streams
whirling with its tangled beauty.

To look at it is to study the past lives of waters,
the meanders: the way water cuts a groove
in the earth and changes it forever.
The river's ghosts snake and bend over time.
It is lovely. Alluvial. The memory of a mighty river
compressed.

At its heart: a jumble of coils and purls
that shapes the soil, constantly repairing the landscape.
A repository for memory preserving a shared moment
as when two people have loved each other well
the topography transforms, diverges over time, cleaves
a clearer path to where it was always meant to go.

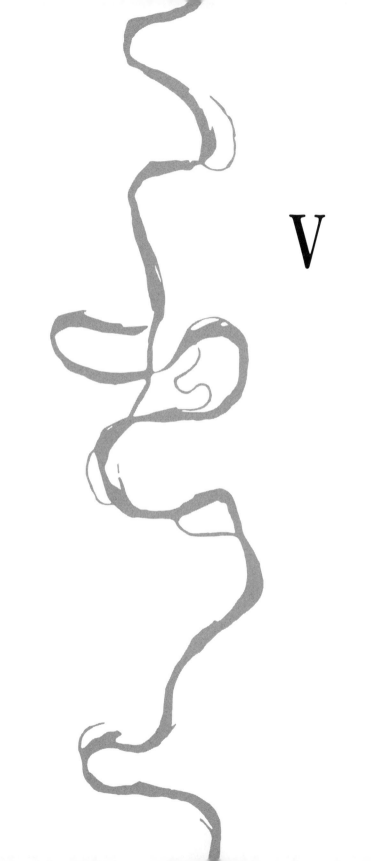

V

For Ella

I love a wild daffodil,
the one that grows
where she's planted—
along a wooded highway
left to its own abandon,
but not abandoned.
Her big yellow head
leaning toward or away
from the sun. Not excluded
but exclusive, her trumpet
heralds no one, not even
the Canada geese—
their long-necked honks
announcing their journey
to somewhere else.
She'll be here less
than a season, grace us
with green slender stems
strong enough to withstand
rain and spring's
early chill.
And when she goes,
what remains
she'll bury deep
inside the bulb of her,
take a part of me with her
until she returns.
How lucky am I
to love this bloom.

Inheritance

My mother never mistook cooking for love—that's not a slight.
She was too practical for that, rotating shifts as a nurse
with my dad the cop so someone was always at home with me.
Canned and processed, she took what her generation gave her:
creamed corn, Beefaroni, orange Kraft cheese slices in perfect
cellophane squares. Miracle Whip not mayonnaise, margarine
instead of butter. It's been a minute since she cooked from scratch:
thick-sliced ham cut up and thrown in a pot of iced potatoes
or butter beans. Deviled eggs and deviled crabs with Krispy Kreme
glazed donuts on the side, Kool-Aid to wash it all down.
No recipes to inherit, no sacred cows to burn on the stove's
bright eye. Provide. Provide. We do the best we can. When I cook,
I speak to her, skillet to skillet, my crab cakes to her fish sticks,
talking between the bones and claws, the hot oil of it all.

Sheltering in Place

The wisteria is in bloom.
      Their sickeningly sweet scent
           carries on the wind as I take

the dog for her morning walk.
      Doesn't seem to bother
           the murmuration of starlings

that take off on our approach,
      shimmer of black diamonds, only to return
           where they once started.

Our closeness makes us vulnerable,
      but it helps to know things are growing,
           thriving. A necessary tension. What lurks

in the tall grass keeps me moving—
      field mouse, antler, tufts of down,
           all that remains from a dove

while the hawk still circles.

Manifesto

You can't eat your cake and have it, too, says my boyfriend
and Ted Kaczynski, turning clichés into bombs. My boyfriend
who is not the Unabomber loves me from 1,300 miles away.
We dream over the phone, count the days until our next visit.
At Whole Foods before Valentine's Day, I buy a red velvet cake
I'll eat alone. A man walks out with a double dozen red roses
wrapped in cellophane. I miss my boyfriend. Can I eat my cake
and have it, too? Transposed verbs are what got Kaczynski caught—
his use of language, his arcane mind, but he wasn't wrong.
What good is having a cake if you can't eat it? That clumsy
phrase comes straight out of Middle English, straight from
my valentine's red mouth. He long-distance laughs as I puzzle
the meaning but isn't that the point? Love is a kind of syntax,
a soft rhyme, prison time. I'm eating my cake and having it, too.

Aubade

My morning walk takes me
down the long path that leads
to the gate. Mabel trots ahead of me
through the mowed lawn, wet with dew.
She looks for rabbits in the hedges,
an unsuspecting robin. The moon visible
in the western horizon,
while the sun makes its slow hot climb
in the opposite sky.
For now, the air is sweet and cool.
Where the road bends
I stop before the magnolia
where a single bud is in bloom:
creamy white, mouth wide as a chalice.
I've stopped asking
what brought me here,
stopped asking for directions.
I am not lost. I move toward
the almost-words a frog speaks
at the pond's edge before it leaps.
I stand one-legged on a gnarled root rising
above the still surface
half-covered in pollen and algae.
Don't say I am untouched
or unremarkable.
No one has been where I am going.
I fly with the blue heron
who takes off as soon as
she's been discovered.

Glitter Road

I'll take my miracles however they appear
these days—a salamander poking its head

above the bricks; the shocking blue overcoat
of the season's first bluebird; a spider web

unbroken. At the corner of Molly Barr
and McElroy I saw a thick trail of glitter

in the curve of the right turn lane. Fuchsia.
Heavy shimmer refracting the noonday sun

as if laying flat a rainbow's extracted hue.
Not paint, or blood, or a parade shedding

its cheer. It's the faded streak of eye shadow
as it trails into flecks, then disappears.

I think of cars passing through this moment—
their undercarriages aglow with possibility.

Hard not to feel good riding a glistening wave,
my tires now bespeckled with a purple sheen

that's tough to rid or wash away, the road ahead
made beautiful by this temporary shine.

Notes

"Narcissi in January"—The line "How deep, how often have I been touched" is from Terrance Hayes's poem "Wind in a Box" from his book of the same title.

"Rebel Rebel"—During the summer of 2020, the Confederate statue at the University of Mississippi's campus entrance was moved to a cemetery overlooking the campus football field.

"Cartwheel"—"My legs cloud-swimming toward the coming world" is a modified line from Major Jackson's poem "Winter" from his collection *The Absurd Man*. His original line: "and legs as though cloud-swimming toward the coming world."

"At the Rededication of the Emmett Till Memorial, Glendora, MS"—The line, "*Every time it's taken down, it's going back up*," is a quote from Jerome Little, founder, Emmett Till Memorial Commission.

"Woman Swallowed by a Python in Her Cornfield"—Poem inspired by the article "Woman Swallowed by Python as She Checked on Her Cornfield" in *Yahoo! Lifestyle:* https://www .yahoo.com/lifestyle/woman-swallowed-python-she-checked -100000564.html

"Three white Ole Miss students use guns to vandalize a memorial to lynching victim Emmett Till"—This is a found poem with text taken from the article, "Ole Miss students dishonored civil rights icon Emmett Till in a 'sacred place,'" July 19, 2019, *USA Today* https://www.usatoday.com/story/opinion/2019/07/26/ole-miss-student-dishonored-civil-rights-icon-emmett-till -column/1840976001/

"From Memory"—The line, "There were nights so simple it was as if the stars came down to sit with us, not saying a word," is from "Parable of a Marriage" from the collection *Not All Saints* by Sean Thomas Dougherty.

"The Map"—Mississippi River Meander Belt #7, Mississippi River Commission, 1947: The map cited in this poem and used as the cover for this book is one of fifteen created by Dr. Harold N. Fisk as part of his work for the US Army Corp of Engineers. In addition to displaying the current course of the Mississippi River, it shows how the meanders have shifted the river over time.

Acknowledgments

My thanks to the editors of the publications where these poems were first published:

32 Poems: "Clit Ode"
Adroit Journal: "Rowan Oak"
APR: "Manifesto," "On the Edge of a Field in Sumner, Mississippi"
ArtFuse: "The Map"
Bennington Review: "Driving through Mississippi after the Capitol Hill Riot," "Woman Swallowed by a Python in Her Cornfield"
Birmingham Review: "What's Left"
The Common: "Autopsy"
Cortland Review: "In the Blue Hour"
Diode: "From Memory," "Narcissi in January"
Green Mountains Review: "The Beyond Place," "Boyfriend Pantoum," "The Great Hello"
Good River Review: "Cheaters"
Kenyon Review Online: "Elation"
Ibbetson Street Press: "Harvest"
Los Angeles Review: "Cartwheel"
Mom Egg Review: "I Take Off My Black Dress," "No Joke" (formerly "Post-Inauguration, 2016")
Muddy River Poetry Review: "Axilla," "Bathtub Graveyard," "I Slept in John Grisham's Bed"
Paterson Literary Review: "At the Rededication of the Emmett Till Memorial"

Ploughshares: "The Morning Before the Rains Came"
Poetry: "Three white Ole Miss students use guns to vandalize a memorial to lynching victim Emmett Till"
Poetry Northwest: "Mississippi Season"
Quasar: "Regret Nothing" (formerly "Poem")
Quarterly West: "Aubade," "Elegy for the End of the World"
Rattle: "What's Love Got to Do with It"
Shenandoah Review: "Begin Again"
SIERRA magazine online: "The River Remembers"
storySouth: "Inheritance," "Low Delta Country"
SWWIM: "For Ella"
Water-Stone Review: "Rebel Rebel"

"Bloom" was published in the anthology *The Eloquent Poem: 128 Contemporary Poems and Their Making* edited by Elise Paschen (New York: Persea, 2019). "Glitter Road" was published in the anthology *Alone Together: Love, Grief, and Comfort During the Time of COVID-19* edited by Jennifer Haupt (Canada: Central Avenue Publishing, 2020).

"At the Rededication of the Emmett Till Memorial" was cowinner of the 2022 Allen Ginsberg Poetry Award. "For Ella" was nominated for a Pushcart by the editors of SWWIM. "I Take Off My Black Dress" was nominated for a Pushcart Prize by *Mom Egg Review*. "Rebel Rebel" was nominated for a Pushcart Prize by the editors of *Water-Stone Review*.

Thank you to the following poets for their friendship and guidance: Joseph O. Legaspi, Cindy Veach, Jennifer Martelli, Susan Rich, Colleen Michaels, Jennifer Jean, J. D. Scrimgeour, Kevin Carey, Dawn Paul, Melissa Ginsburg, Kelli Russell Agodon, and Keetje Kuipers.

Thanks to CavanKerry Press for their hard work and dedication to poetry. In particular: Gabriel Cleveland, Dimitri Reyes, Joy Arbor, and Baron Wormser, who has worked with me on four (!) books. Gratitude to Heather Brown of Mind the Bird Media. Simply the best!

Special thanks to Salem State University, Mass Poetry, Mass Cultural Council, Mass Center for the Book, Creative Collective, and the Thursday Poets for their continued support. Shout out to Jen Benka and the Poetry Coalition for being ferocious advocates for poets and poetry.

My undying gratitude to the MFA Program at the University of Mississippi Oxford. My time as the John and Renée Grisham Writer in Residence gave me the space to fully envision this book. To the UM's stellar faculty, past and present: Aimee Nezhukumatathil, Beth Ann Fennelly, Derrick Harriell, Melissa Ginsburg, Matt Bondurant, Ann Fisher-Wirth, Dustin Parsons, Chris Offutt, Kiese Laymon, and Ivo Kamps—thank you.

To Mom and Dad, Ella and Alex: I love you.
To Mabel: *Good girl!*
To Cade Smith: Thank you for our Mississippi season.

CavanKerry's Mission

A not-for-profit literary press serving art and community, Cavan-Kerry is committed to expanding the reach of poetry and other fine literature to a general readership by publishing works that explore the emotional and psychological landscapes of everyday life, and to bringing that art to the underserved where they live, work, and receive services.

Other Books in the Notable Voices Series

Losing Season, Jack Ridl

Without Wings, Laurie Lamon

An Apron Full of Beans: New and Selected Poems, Sam Cornish

The Poetry Life: Ten Stories, Baron Wormser

BEAR, Karen Chase

Fun Being Me, Jack Wiler

Common Life, Robert Cording

The Origins of Tragedy & Other Poems, Kenneth Rosen

Apparition Hill, Mary Ruefle

Against Consolation, Robert Cording

This book was printed on paper from responsible sources.

Glitter Road was typeset in Garamond Premier Pro by Adobe senior type designer Robert Slimbach. It is a practical, 21st-century update to Claude Garamond's metal punches and book types originally created in the mid-1500s, considered to be the pinnacle of beauty and practicality in typefounding.